NOTE-FOR-NOTE
KEYBOARD
TRANSCRIPTIONS

ACOUSTIC
PIANO BALLADS

2nd Edition

T0059266

ISBN 0-634-09046-1

HAL•LEONARD®
CORPORATION
7777 W. BLUEMOUND RD. P.O. BOX 13819 MILWAUKEE, WI 53213

Visit Hal Leonard Online at
www.halleonard.com

ABOUT THIS BOOK

When playing through the transcriptions in this book, it is important to consider the following:

1. *The primary keyboard part always appears directly below the vocal line.*

2. *Any secondary keyboard parts appear below the primary keyboard part. The instrument sound is always indicated in the measure in which the part is first played. (Sound changes are also indicated where appropriate.)*

3. *Other prominent instrumental parts, such as string and horn lines, are also included. It is important to note that these parts are arranged so that they may be played as secondary keyboard parts. The pitches are accurate; however, the voicings of the chords may be modified to be more indicative of a keyboard approach.*

4. *If there is no keyboard part on the recording for an extended time, other instrumental parts are often arranged to be played by the primary keyboard part. These sections are optional and are intended to be played only if the actual instruments (such as guitar) are not available.*

5. *"Fill" boxes are sometimes included when a particular fill, or figure, is played on the repeat or D.S. only. A typical indication would be "Play Fill 1 (2nd time)."*

The transcriptions in this book are useful in a variety of situations: with a band, with a sequencer, with a CD, or solo playing. Whatever your purpose, you can now play your favorite songs just as the artists recorded them.

CONTENTS

Angel

Words and Music by Sarah McLachlan

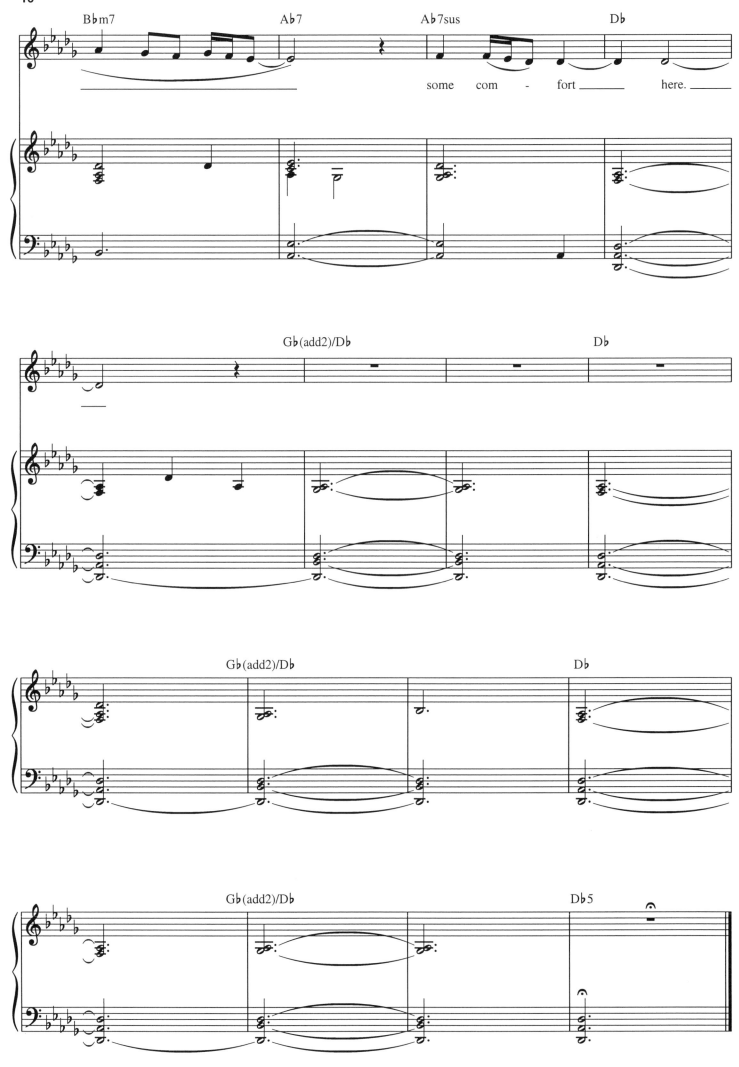

some com - fort ___ here. ___

Don't Let the Sun Go Down on Me

Words and Music by Elton John and Bernie Taupin

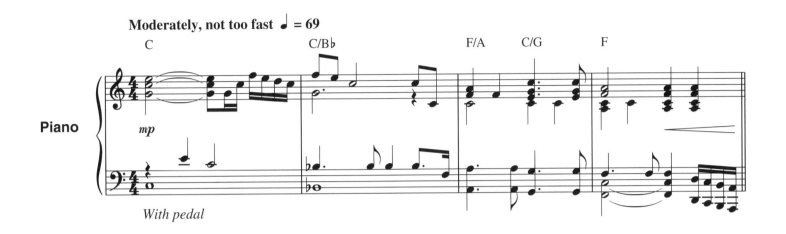

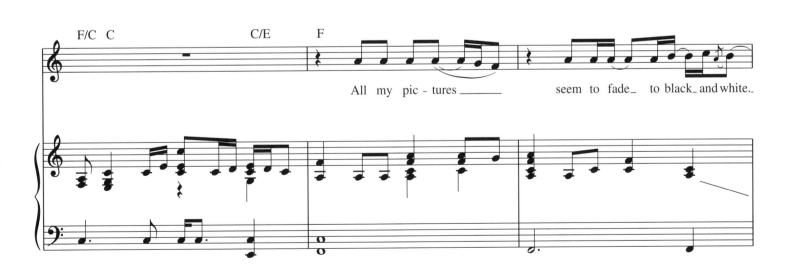

but los-ing eve-ry-thing ___ is like the

To Coda ⊕

sun go-ing down on ___ me.

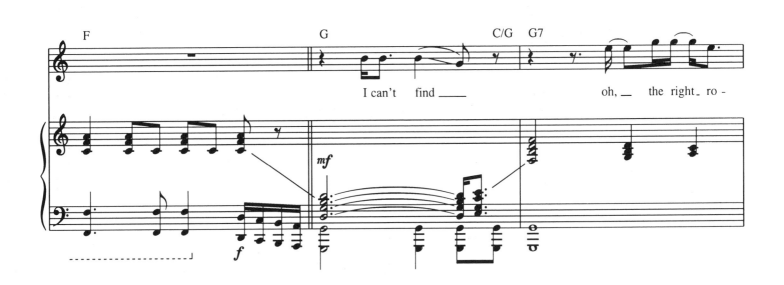

I can't find ___ oh, ___ the right ro-

Al - though I search my-self, it's al - ways __ some-one else I see. __

I'd just al - low a frag - ment of __ your life __ to wan - der free, __

__ yeah, _____ but

Candle in the Wind

Music by Elton John
Words by Bernie Taupin

know-in' who to cling to when the rain set in.

I would have liked to have known you, but I was just

a kid. Your can - dle burned out long be - fore

your leg - end ev - er did.

*Synthesizer (pad) doubles Piano part.

24

leg - end ev - er did.

Good-bye, Nor - ma Jean.

Though I nev - er knew you __ at all, you had the grace to

Endless Love
from ENDLESS LOVE
Words and Music by Lionel Richie

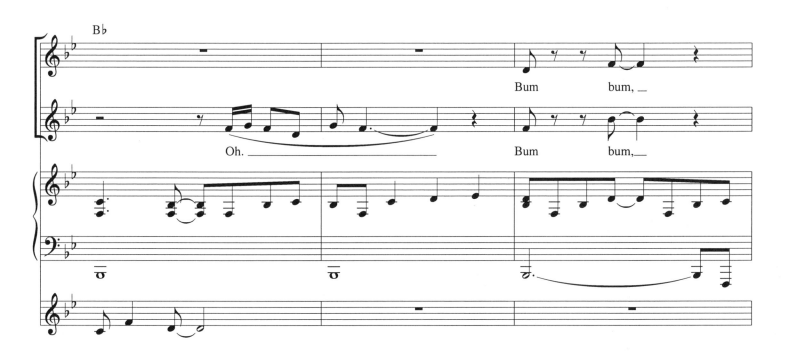

40

give _____ it all to you, _____ my love, my love,

give _____ it all to you, my love, _____

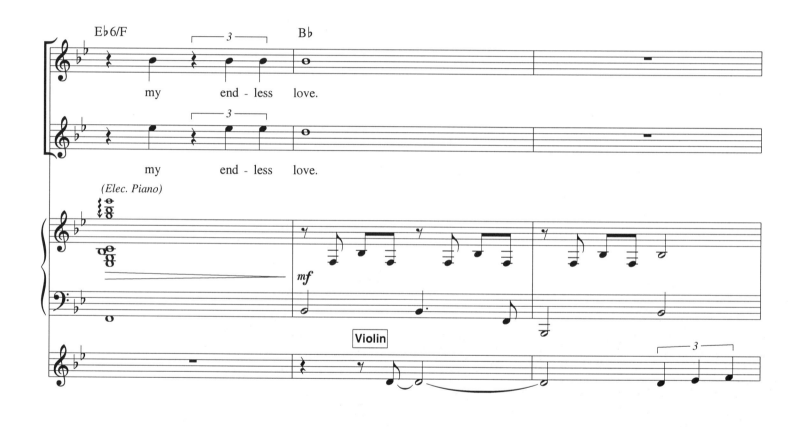

my end-less love.

my end-less love.

(Elec. Piano)

Violin

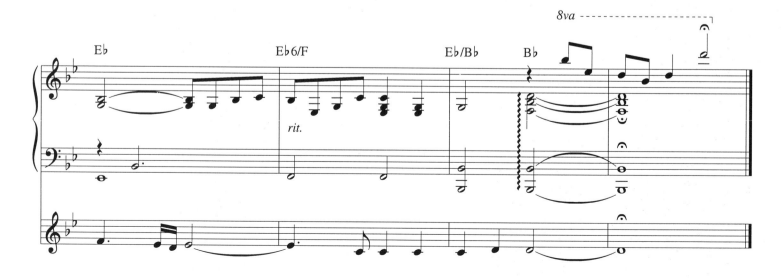

rit.

8va

Imagine

Words and Music by John Lennon

I-mag-ine there's _ no heav-en;
I-mag-ine there's _ no coun - tries;
I-mag-ine no ____ pos - ses - sions; _

it's eas - y if you try._____
it is - n't hard ___ to do._____
I won-der if you can. _____

It's Too Late

Words and Music by Carole King and Toni Stern

One of us __ is chang-in',   or may-be we've just __ stopped __ try - in'. __
you look so __ un-hap-py   and I feel _____ like   a fool. _____

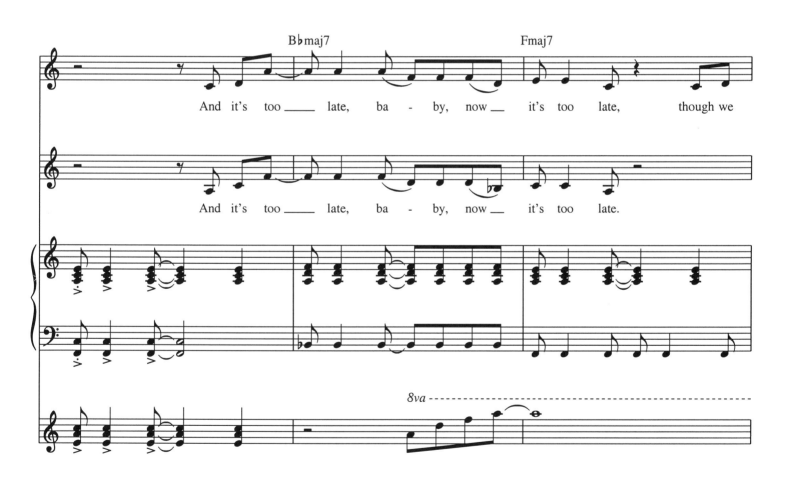

And it's too _____ late, ba - by, now __ it's too late,   though we
And it's too _____ late, ba - by, now __ it's too late.

Fill

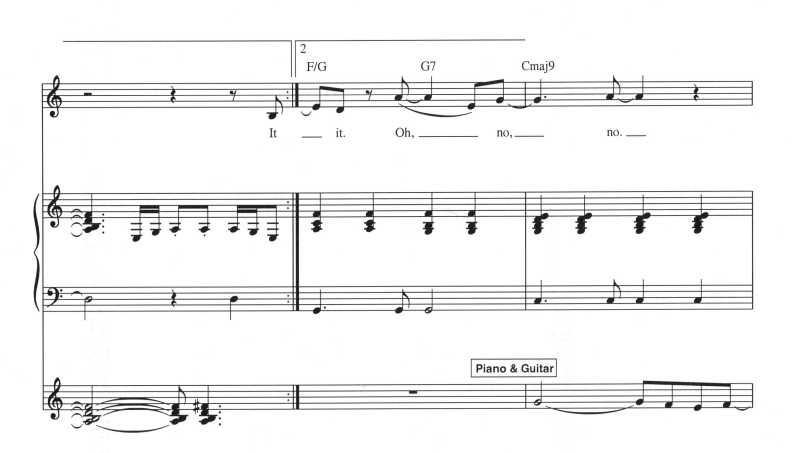

Doo doo doo doo doo doo doo doo __ doo doo. __

Doo doo doo doo doo doo doo doo. __

Guitar solo - ad lib.

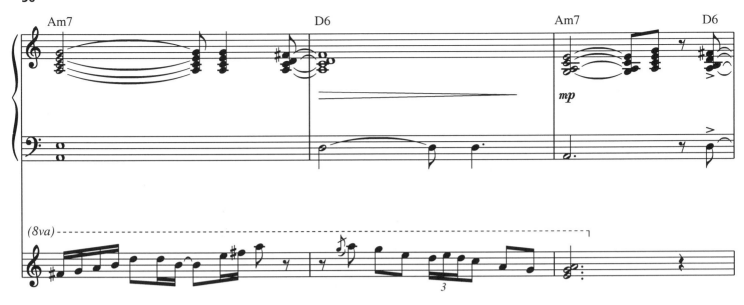

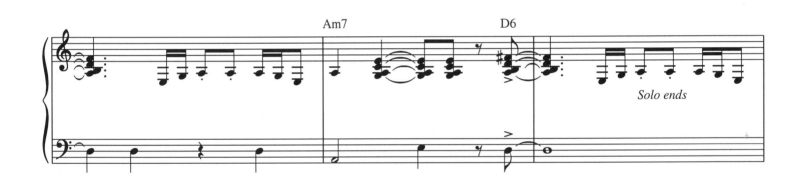

There'll be good times _ a - gain for me and _ you, _ but we just can't stay to-geth - er; don't _ you

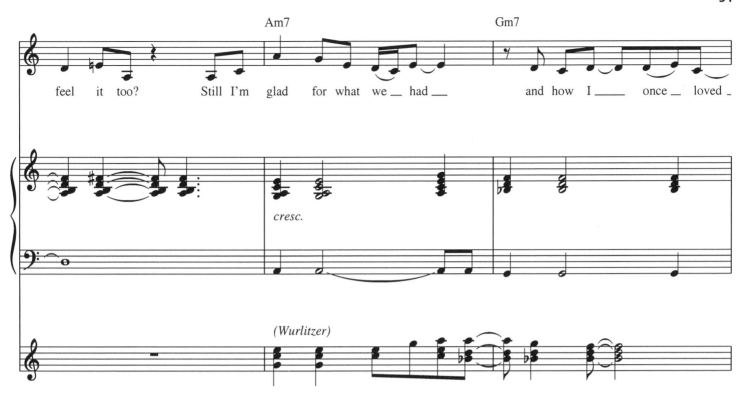

feel it too? Still I'm glad for what we __ had __ and how I __ once __ loved __

__ you.

But it's too __ late, ba - by, now __

But it's too __ late, ba - by, now __

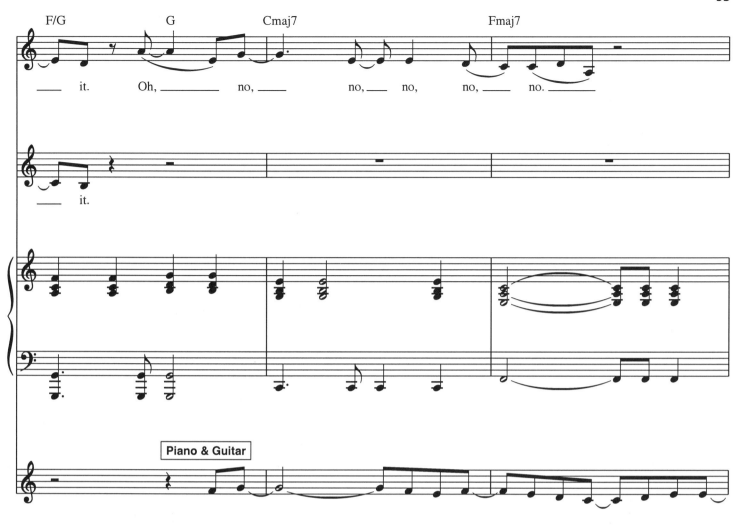

It's too late, _____ ba - by, it's too __ late_

_____ now, _ dar - lin', it's too __ late. _____

It's too __ late. _____

Mandy

Words and Music by Scott English and Richard Kerr

Let It Be

Words and Music by John Lennon and Paul McCartney

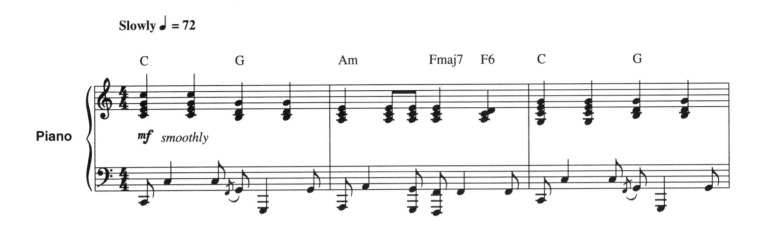

When I find my-self_ in times_ of trou-ble Moth-er Ma - ry comes_ to me,

speak-ing words of wis - dom, let it be.____ And in my hour of dark - ness she is stand-

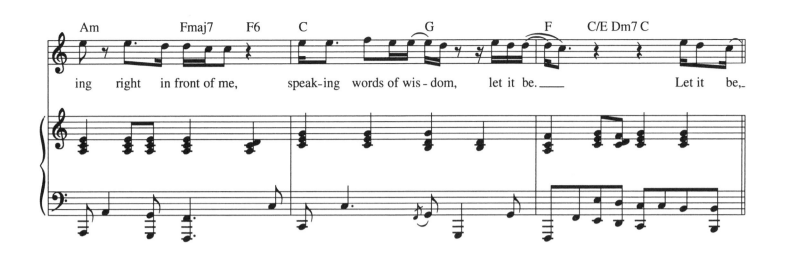

ing right in front of me, speak-ing words of wis-dom, let it be. ____ Let it be,_

____ let it be, let it be, ____ let it be._ Whis-per words_ of wis-dom, let it be._

Organ

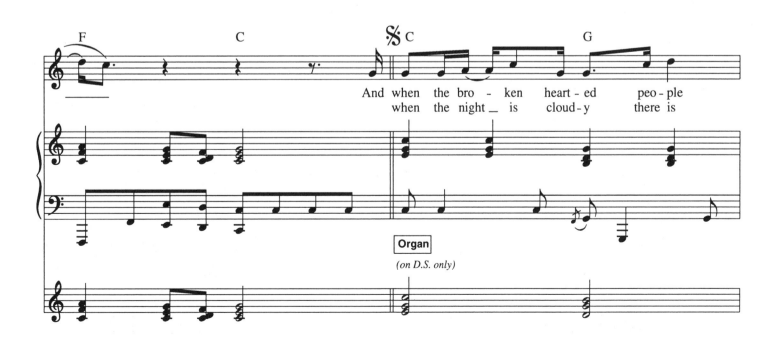

And when the bro - ken heart - ed peo - ple
when the night _ is cloud-y there is

Organ
(on D.S. only)

66

Sailing

Words and Music by Christopher Cross

70

ry me, and soon I will be free.

To Coda

Fantasy, it gets the best of me

when I'm sail - ing.

She's Got a Way

Words and Music by Billy Joel

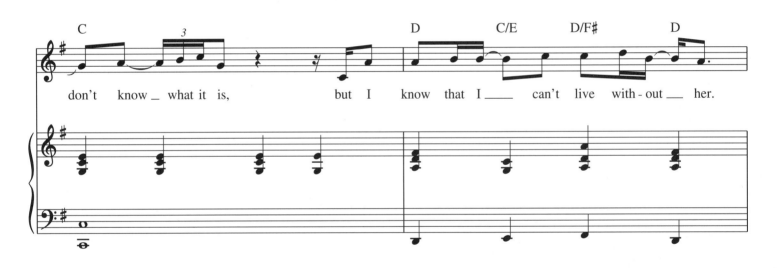

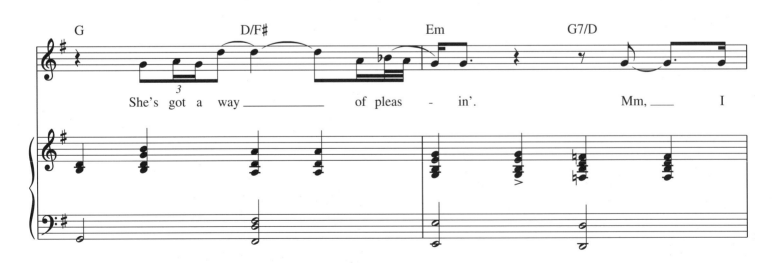

So Far Away

Words and Music by Carole King

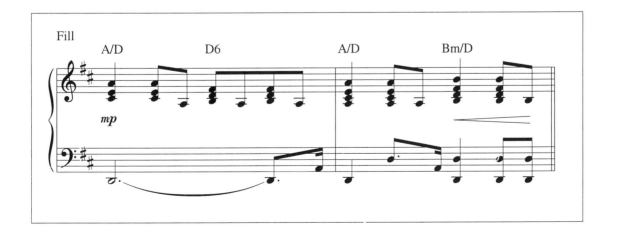

a - way!__

(a - way!)

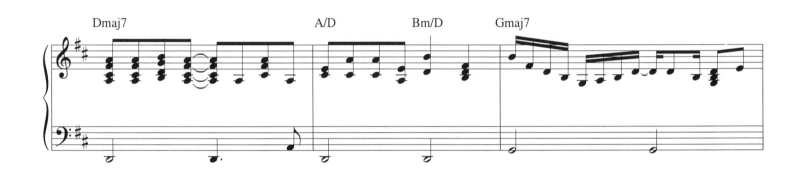

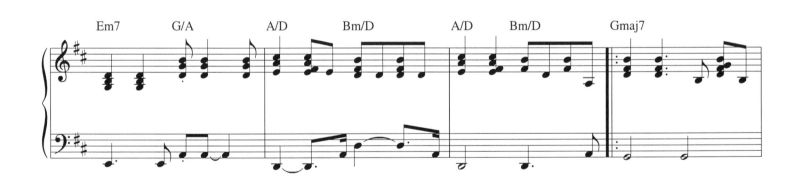

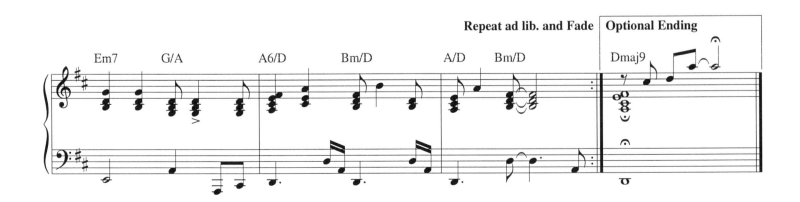

Tapestry

Words and Music by Carole King

* The original recording contains two separate piano parts. For this arrangement, they have been combined to be playable as a solo.

come ___ to take me back.

You Never Give Me Your Money

Words and Music by John Lennon and Paul McCartney

Fmaj7   Bm7♭5   E7   1. Am

and in the mid-dle of ne-go-ti-a-tions you break down. ___
and in the mid-dle of in-ves-ti-ga-tion I

2. Am   C/G   G

break down. ___

Slightly faster (♩♩ = ♪ ♪♪)

C   E   Am   C7

Out of col-lege, mon-ey spent,   see no fu-ture, pay no rent,

Honky-Tonk Piano

f

F   G7   C

all the mon-ey's gone, ___ no-where to go. ___

An - y job - ber got the sack, Mon - day morn - ing turn-ing back,

yel-low lor - ry slow, __ no - where to go. __ But oh, __

__ that mag - ic feel-ing, no - where to go.

Elect. Guitar and Bass

8vb

Oh, that mag - ic feel-ing, no - where to go, __ no-where to go. __

(8vb)

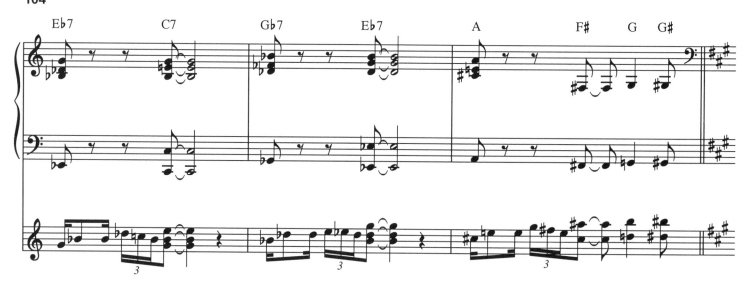

One sweet dream,

Rhythm Guitar and Bass

pick up the bags, get in the lim - ou - sine. __

You've Got a Friend

Words and Music by Carole King

(Play L.H. in octaves 2nd time)

Bbm7   Cm7

bright - en up   e -   ven your dark - est   night.__
soon   you'll hear me knock - in'   at   your   door.__

Play Fill 1 (2nd time)

cresc.

Db/Eb   Eb   Db/Eb   Eb7sus

You   just   call

Ab

out my __ name,   and you know

mf

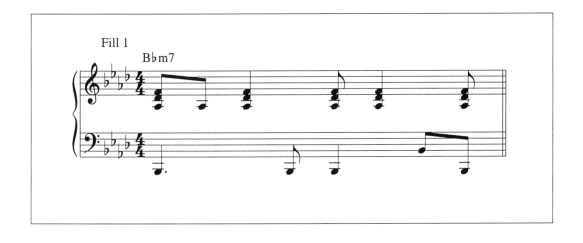

Fill 1

Bbm7

Your Song

Words and Music by Elton John and Bernie Taupin

I'd buy ___ a big house where ___ we both ___ could
it's for peo - ple like you where that ___ keep it ___ turned ___

live. ___
— on. ___

If I was a sculp - tor, heh,
So ex - cuse me for - get - ting,

Sing Vocal Fill (2nd time)

but then a - gain, ___ no, or a man who makes po - tions in ___ a
but these things I do. You see, I've for - got - ten ___ if they're green

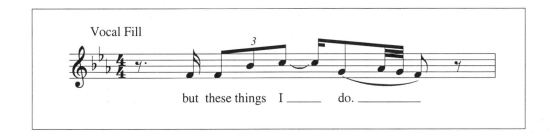

Vocal Fill

but these things I ___ do. ___

Ribbon in the Sky

Words and Music by Stevie Wonder

122

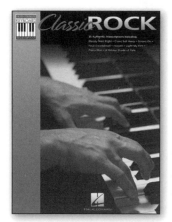